D1195396

THE
Tiny Journalist

Naomi Shihab Nye

THE
Tiny Journalist

POEMS

American Poets Continuum Series, No. 170

BOA Editions, Ltd. ❧ Rochester, NY ❧ 2019

First Edition
19 20 21 22 7 6 5 4 3 2 1

For information about permission to reuse any material from this book, please contact
The Permissions Company at www.permissionscompany.com or e-mail permdude@
gmail.com.

Publications by BOA Editions, Ltd.—a not-for-profit corporation
under section 501 (c) (3) of the United States Internal Revenue
Code—are made possible with funds from a variety of sources,
including public funds from the Literature Program of the Na-
tional Endowment for the Arts; the New York State Council on
the Arts, a state agency; and the County of Monroe, NY. Private
funding sources include the Max and Marian Farash Charitable
Foundation; the Mary S. Mulligan Charitable Trust; the Roches-
ter Area Community Foundation; the Ames-Amzalak Memorial
Trust in memory of Henry Ames, Semon Amzalak, and Dan
Amzalak; and contributions from many individuals nationwide. See Colophon on page
124 for special individual acknowledgments.

ART WORKS.
arts.gov

State of the Arts

NYSCA

Cover Design: Sandy Knight
Cover Art: "House with Two Gardens" by Christina Brinkman
Interior Design and Composition: Richard Foerster
BOA Logo: Mirko

Library of Congress Cataloging-in-Publication Data

Names: Nye, Naomi Shihab, author.
Title: The tiny journalist : poems / Naomi Shihab Nye.
Description: First edition. | Rochester, NY : BOA Editions, Ltd., [2019] |
  Series: American poets continuum series, ; no. 170 | Includes index.
Identifiers: LCCN 2018050933 (print) | LCCN 2018055328 (ebook) | ISBN
  9781942683841 (ebook) | ISBN 9781942683728 (hardcover : alk. paper) |
  ISBN 9781942683735 (pbk. : alk. paper)
Subjects: LCSH: American poetry—Women authors—21st century.
Classification: LCC PS3564.Y44 (ebook) | LCC PS3564.Y44 A6 2019 (print) | DDC
  811/.54—dc23
LC record available at https://lccn.loc.gov/2018050933

BOA Editions, Ltd.
250 North Goodman Street, Suite 306
Rochester, NY 14607
www.boaeditions.org
A. Poulin, Jr., Founder (1938–1996)

In memory
May Mansoor Munn
author of *Where Do Dreams and Dreaming Go?*
A Palestinian Quaker in America

And in honor of Janna Jihad Ayyad
and her cousin Ahed Tamimi—
all young people devoted to justice
and sharing their voices.

✺

"We will never give up in the peace place,
in the Holy Land, we'll see the peace one day."
　　　　　　　　　　—Janna Jihad Ayyad

". . . I am particularly inspired by the people of Gaza
who put all of us to shame with their resilience and steadfastness."
　　　　　　　　　　—Sani Meo, Publisher, *This Week in Palestine*

"From presidents Truman to Trump, US administrations have never
actually been 'an honest broker' of peace between Palestinians and
Israelis, regardless of all the rhetoric and official positions."
　　　　　　　　　　—Mohamed Mohamed, *Palestine Center Brief No. 320*

"Revived bitterness
is unnecessary unless
　　One is ignorant."
　　　　　　　　　　—Marianne Moore, American poet

"Apartheid means fundamentalist clergy spearheading the deepening
of segregation, inequality, supremacism, and subjugation.
　　Apartheid means . . . separate, segregated roads and highways for
Israelis and Palestinians in the West Bank.
　　Apartheid means hundreds of attacks by settlers targeting
Palestinian property, livelihoods, and lives, without convictions,
charges, or even suspects. Apartheid means uncounted Palestinians
jailed without trial, shot dead without trial, shot dead in the back
while fleeing and without just cause.
　　Apartheid means Israeli officials using the army, police, military
courts, and draconian administrative detentions, not only to head off
terrorism, but to curtail nearly every avenue of non-violent protest
available to Palestinians."
　　　　　　　　　　—Bradley Burston, *Haaretz*, 2015

✺

Author's Note:

My father's Palestinian family, refugees from their Jerusalem home after 1948, lived in a village not far from Nabi Saleh village, where Janna Jihad Ayyad and her family live. I lived between Jerusalem and Ramallah as a teenager and witnessed many of the struggles firsthand, which have unfortunately only heightened and intensified in the succeeding years. It is important to clarify that these poems or sections thereof are not Janna's actual words. They are "my" words, imagining Janna's circumstances via her Facebook postings and my own personal and collective knowledge of the situation she was born into and lives with on a daily basis. So the texts presented here are a blending of stories—my father's, Janna's, my ongoing research, and my own personal experience living there and on many subsequent journeys. In the way of all poetry, hopefully it gets something true or right.

Also:

Since Palestinians are also Semites, being pro-justice
for Palestinians is never an anti-Semitic position, no matter what
anybody says.

Contents

I.

II.

I.

Morning Song

For Janna

The tiny journalist
will tell us what she sees.

Document the moves, the dust,
soldiers blocking the road.

Yes, she knows how to take a picture
with her phone. Holds it high

like a balloon. Yes, she would
prefer to dance and play,

would prefer the world
to be pink. It is her job to say

what she sees, what is happening.
From her vantage point everything

is huge—but don't look down on her.
She's bigger than you are.

If you stomp her garden
each leaf expands its view.

Don't hide what you do.
She sees you at 2 a.m. adjusting your

impenetrable vest.
What could she have

that you want? Her treasures,
the shiny buttons her grandmother loved.

Her cousin, her uncle.
There might have been a shirt . . .

The tiny journalist notices
action on far away roads

farther even than the next village.
She takes counsel from bugs so

puffs of dust find her first.
Could that be a friend?

They pretended not to see us.
They came at night with weapons.

What was our crime? That we liked
respect as they do? That we have pride?

She stares through a hole in the fence,
barricade of words and wire,

feels the rising fire
before anyone strikes a match.

She has a better idea.

Moon over Gaza

I am lonely
for my friends.
They liked me,
trusted my coming.
I think they looked up at me
more than other people do.

I who have been staring down so long
see no reason for the sorrows humans make.
I dislike the scuffle of bombs blasting
very much. It blocks my view.

A landscape of grieving
feels different afterwards.
Different sheen from a simple desert,
rubble of walls, silent children who once said
my name like a prayer.

Sometimes I am bigger than
a golden plate,
a giant coin,
and everyone gasps.

Maybe it is wrong
that I am so calm.

Exotic Animals, Book for Children

Armadillo means
"little armored one."
Some of us become this to survive
in our own countries.
I would like to see an armadillo
crossing the road.
Our armor is invisible,
it polishes itself.
We might have preferred to be
a softer animal, wouldn't you?
With fur and delicate paws,
like an African Striped Grass Mouse,
also known as Zebra Mouse.

Janna

At 7, making videos.
At 10, raising the truth flag.
At 11, raising it higher,
traveling to South Africa,
keffiyah knotted on shoulders,
interviews in airports.
Please, could you tell us . . .

You know gazing into a camera
can be a bridge, so you stare
without blinking.
People drift to the sides of the film,
don't want to be noticed,
put on the spot.
You know the spot is the only thing
that matters.
What else? Long days,
tired trousers pinned
on roof lines,
nothing good expected.

It's right in front of me,
I didn't go looking for it.
We're living in the middle of trouble.
No reason not to say it straight.
They do not consider us equal.
They blame us for everything,
forgetting what they took,
how they took it.
We are made of bone and flesh and story
but they poke their big guns
into our faces
and our front doors
and our living rooms

as if we are vapor.
Why can't they see
how beautiful we are?

The saddest part?
We all could have had
twice as many friends.

Separation Wall

When the milk is sour,
it separates.

The next time you stop speaking,
ask yourself why you were born.

They say they are scared of us.
The nuclear bomb is scared of the cucumber.

When my mother asks me to slice cucumbers,
I feel like a normal person with fantastic dilemmas:

Do I make rounds or sticks? Shall I trim the seeds?
I ask my grandmother if there was ever a time

she felt like a normal person every day,
not in danger, and she thinks for as long

as it takes a sun to set and says, Yes.
I always feel like a normal person.

They just don't see me as one.
We would like the babies not to find out about

the failures waiting for them. I would like
them to believe on the other side of the wall

is a circus that just hasn't opened yet. Our friends,
learning how to juggle, to walk on tall poles.

Dareen Said Resist

And went to jail.
We were asking, What?
You beat us with butts of guns
for years,
tear-gas our grandmas,
and you can't take
Resist?

In Northern Ireland They Called It "The Troubles"

What do we call it?
The very endless nightmare?
The toothache of tragedy?

I call it the life no one would choose.
To be always on guard,
never secure,
jumping when a skillet drops.

I watch the babies finger their
cups and spoons and think
they don't know yet.
They don't know how empty

the cup of hope can feel.
Here in the land of tea and coffee
offered on round trays a million times
a day, still a thirst so great

you could die every night, longing
for a better life.

How Long?

The tiny journalist
is growing taller very quickly.
She's adding breadth, depth,
to every conversation,
asking different questions, not just

Who What When Where Why?
but How long? How can it be?
What makes this seem right to you?

Even when she isn't present,
she might be taping from the trees.

What happened to you in the twentieth century?
Remember? We never forgot about it. You did.

Rounded up at gunpoint, our people
brutally beaten, pummeled in prisons,
massacred for a rumor of stones.

Once there was a stuffed squash
who didn't wish to be eaten.
Kousa habibti, pine nuts for eyes.
I dreamed about her when I was five.
She helped me start my mission.

For Palestine

In memory, Fr. Gerry Reynolds of Belfast, "Let us pray for Palestine"

How lonely the word PEACE is becoming.
Missing her small house under the olive trees.

The grandmothers carried her in a bucket when
they did their watering.
She waited for them in the sunrise,
then fell back into reach. Whole lives unfolded.
The uncles tucked her into suit coat pockets
after buttoning white shirts for another day.
Fathers, mothers, babies
heard her whispering in clouds over Palestine,
mingling softly, making a promise,
sending her message to the ground.
It wasn't a secret.
Things will calm down soon, she said.
Hold your head up. Don't forget.
When Ahed went to prison, we shook
our tired hands in the air and wept.
Young girl dreaming of a better world!
Don't shoot her cousins, my cousins, our cousins.
Wouldn't you slap for that?
It was only a slap.

The word Peace a ticket elsewhere for some.
People dreamed night and day of calmer lives.
Maybe Peace would be their ticket back too.
They never threw away that hope. Karmic wheel,
great myth of fairness kept spinning . . .
I dreamed of Ahed's hair.

When I was born, they say
a peaceful breeze lilted the branches—

my first lullaby. The temperature dropped.
A voice pressed me forward,
told me to speak.
Being raised in a house of stories with garlic
gave me courage.
Everything began, *Far, far away. Long, long ago.*
And everything held us close.
Is this your story, or mine?
Olive oil lives in a dented can with a long spout.

What happens to Peace when people fight?
(She hides her face.)
What does she dream of?
(Better people.)
Does she ever give up?

Sometimes she feels very lonely on the earth.
She wants to walk openly with children.
Live the way they might.
Have a party with white cookies on simple plates.
Lots of them.
Nuts chopped fine.
She wants everyone to share.

Small People

Janna says the camera is stronger than the gun.
"I can send my message to small people
and they send it to others."
Sun improving consciousness.
Wind ruffling discomfort.

Janna, we are small indeed.
Weighing the word "dream"
as it slips through midnight air.
Small people keeping it alive.

Help us ride on every train
to better history. Weighing
"fog" and "suitcase," weighing "tomorrow"—
before we know two words in this life,
we're already missing
what already left.

Women in Black

I would be one when I grew up.
Hovering, so watchful outside
government buildings, black T-shirts,
black jackets and scarves and gowns—
till then I am a girl in stripes.

They hold a belief—we could all
get along—Arabs, Jews, Swedes,
people with candles, or without.
Even if taunted or hit by stones,
rubber bullets,
we would keep watching,
No Violence!
No War! Trying to be more like
the peaceful village oasis,
Wahat al-Salaam, Nevi Shalom—
half-and-half everything,
school administrators, village counselors,
grocers, gardeners, kids, founded by
a Christian Brother,
why couldn't all villages be like that?
What is wrong with us?

I flip the pages of the tattered Benetton catalogue
my friend's mother still keeps in a drawer—
from before we were born,
Arabs and Jews as true friends
on every page, real people
telling their stories, you could not tell which
is which—aren't there more?

Surely there are more. Red plastic chairs
sitting outside stone and stucco houses,
waiting for us. Waiting for us to sit together.

A project called UNHATE vs. guns.
Which would you choose?
But look how many guns!

Who did this to us?
Money? Guilt?
People in other countries did this to us?
Some people carrying guns look 12 years old.

My father always told me beware of righteousness.
If you are too right, everyone else is wrong.
Illegal settlements creep up the hills at night
erasing our old villages. Boxy white houses
with red roofs marching toward
our old stone terraces. Would you like that?
Americans, would you?

Women in Black don't carry brooms
but I want them to sweep away our pain.
Here by the hills where angels once appeared,
my mother heard of a journalist who answered
How to solve this dilemma?
by saying, Put everything in the hands of women!
Women in black, women in white.
The men had their chance and failed.
Sure, a few women like Golda
said Palestinians didn't exist—
she must have had bad eyesight.
So many voices without a chance yet.
Mine, for example.
It is our turn now.

And That Mysterious Word Holy

You might as well take a rotten lemon,
squeeze it in your hand.
Let the juice trickle down your wrist and arm,
sharp bite of acidity prickling your
scratches and scars and say,
I bow down to you.
When the almond tree erupts into
blossom without help from any people—
I bow down. Here we are in the land
of sacred story, chant, shrines,
altars and grottoes, parables,
and soldiers in camouflage are carrying guns.
What does that say about holy?
How much power it doesn't have—
Thou shalt not kill crumpled under our feet.
Whose religion would you follow?
And why do they wear camouflage?
We can still see them.
Who are they hiding from?
The guns are bigger than we are.
The tanks are bigger than shrines.
Tear gas canisters, grenade casings
littering graves of our ancestors in the cemetery.
I bow down. You bow to the big shining platter
everyone eats off together. Sit in a circle
for your holy rice. Speak after me.
Holy eggplant, my best angel.

Netanyahu

You don't need a periscope
  or a microscope
to see another human being
  guiding a child
    hand on shoulder of child
  arranging coverlet over sleeping child—

You don't need a stethoscope
  to imagine a heartbeat.

What does it mean when one person thinks
  others deserve nothing?
    What is that called?

If you know what it is called, why keep
  doing it?

You don't need a skewer for broiling
    or a paring knife for seeing inside.

Studying English

COURAGE
has age
in it
but I say
age is not required.

A man from Scotland came to visit,
brought us square, buttery cookies,
repeated *Steady at the tiller,*
when he wandered our streets.
I had to search for the
meaning. *Keeping control*
of a situation, staying firm,
phrase often used in seafaring context,
though we have no boats, no rudders,
but originally the phrase connected to
a felled tree, of which we have plenty.

Losing as Its Own Flower

What if we had just said, OK we lose.
How would they have treated us then?

I ask my people, they gasp,
and all have different answers.
No, no, we can never give up.
Stay strong, keep speaking truth.
Truth unfolds in the gardens,
massive cabbages, succulent tomatoes,
orange petals billowing,
even when the drought is long.
Hang on tightly to what we have,
though just a scrap.

The ancestors would be ashamed
if we gave up. The invaders said our land
was barren and sad.
They said we were anti-Semitic.
But we were Semites too.
What could we do?

Giving up is different from losing.

In a way, we did lose. Where is everybody?
Scattered around the world like pollen.
Disappeared into the sunset.
Mingling with other cultures
in the great bubbling stew of the world.

See, we are good at that, why couldn't we
have done better with our invaders?
They came pretending we were
an alien species. Said they had deep ties here,
some of them did, but what about ours?

Why couldn't we all have ties?
They said God said.
(Always trouble.)

We replied, See the stone stoop of my house
with my rubbed footprints in it
after all these years?
See my shining key?

They said we made everything up.
We were crazy.
Is losing worse than being called crazy?

So we did lose. We lost our rhythm of regular living.

You want the page to be clean.
The day wide open, nobody suffering.
We lost our bearings, their voices
blew hard on us, trying to erase,
turning us inside out in their minds,

changing what we became.
Tried to make the world see us that way too.
We were the undeserving.
See what people do?
We could live up to their lies if
they made us crazy enough.
So we did lose.

Professors, educated students, best maker of *maklouba*,
math students of Gaza, embroiderers of the West Bank,
lemon vendors, grapefruit-growers,
artist who stayed in her room painting egg cartons
for so many days, where are you?
(She went to Italy.)

I too dream of Italy, France, Greece.
A village climbing a hill
where I'm not always looking back
over my shoulder,
eyes aren't tipping to the sides
to catch approaching tanks and jeeps,
but this is my job.

Before speech, a baby makes a cat-cry.
Maybe I knew even then.
To document. To pay attention.
We wore striped T-shirts, they wore camouflage.
To be with my family on our ground.

If you live like a real human being—
that is the issue. Not winning and hunting others.
Not dominating.
Not sending your sewage their direction.
Did you know? Did you know they do this?
Not just refusing to lose.

Pink

The grandfather said he wouldn't die
and then he died
which is why
I am staring so hard into the sunset

Mothers Waiting for Their Sons

One boy on the horizon.
A boy is a mountain.
Mother waiting for the moment
when his face comes into sight.
He's dubious about so much hugging now
but the hands, clutched together,
mother and son, still a perfect fit.
Like a mountain when you sit on it.

"ISRAELIS LET BULLDOZERS GRIND TO HALT"

American newspaper headline on the Internet

As if the bulldozers had their own lives
and were just being bulldozers
crushing houses
schoolrooms
clinics
art galleries
whole worlds
on their own time
no people involved.

"Deadline for Demolition"
as if cruelty had its own calendar
a banker or a businessman.

I am mad about language
covering pain
big bandage
masking the wound
let let let
but underneath
the hot blood clotting.

Harvest

The American doctors come to see
what we are living through when we pick olives.
They stand as witnesses, in circles in the grove.
They help hold the ladders.

The doctors say they are shocked to see.
We don't know what it would feel like,
not having guns pointed at us. Guns
have been pointed at us all our lives.

America, don't act surprised, you bought them!
Just tell us how to be a farmer, with guns.
Or celebrate a birthday, with guns.
No guns invited!

The doctors say they will go home and tell
what they experienced. Their kindness is
a balm. Don't people know already?
Where is that news?

Some say Israel would be happiest
if we just disappeared. Like in a magic show?
Our magic is that we are
still here and were always here.

Shadow

Some people feel lost inside their days.
Always waiting for worse to happen.
They make bets with destiny.
My funniest uncle gave up cursing bad words
inside his head. He says he succeeded
one whole hour. He tried to unsubscribe to
the universe made by people. He slept outside
by himself on top of the hill.

When Facebook says I have "followers"—
I hope they know I need their help.
Subscribe to plants, animals, stars,
music, the baby who can't walk yet but
stands up holding on to the sides of things,
tables, chairs, and takes a few clumsy steps,
then sits down hard. This is how we live.

Dead Sea

You could call it a friend, holding you
in its salty palm, letting you feel lighter
on the planet thanks to salt, playing its
joke. I love its somber gray sheen,
its loneliness. It might have preferred
to be a cool wave, an icy Arctic lake,
or the burbling spring my grandmother listened to
her whole childhood before the settlers
drained it off from us. She says the spring
had secrets and knew where jewels were,
in a house nobody lived in, and only children
would ever find the key.

Tattoo

When I hear about "forgotten people" I think,
they are not forgotten by me.
I knew the man down the alley by the market
who dragged his leg. He was out there, smoking,
almost my whole life.

His blue tattered pants,
the small denim pouch like a pocket
around his neck.
It didn't make sense,
but he was always smiling,
if you nodded at him, or not,
chattering words to
a patience prayer, over and over.
It sounded more like Aramaic than Arabic.
He seemed happier to drag somewhere,
the short stone wall under the trees,
than people who find it easy to get there.

On his arm, the tattoo of a skinny blue moon.
He said it was the moon people like least
so he was going to like it most. Fingernail
flicker, little boat, holy symbol
without the star. Are you going to get a tattoo?
he used to tease the kids. We all said, No!
But he is tattooed on my mind
since he disappeared.
He rises in the darkest sky.

Sometimes There Is a Day

Sometimes there is a day you just want
to get so far away from.
Feel it shrink inside you like an island,
as if you were on a boat.
I always wish to be on a boat.
Then, maybe, no more fighting
about land. I want that day to feel
as if it never happened, when Ahmad was burned,
when people were killed, when my cousin was shot.
The day someone went to jail
is not a day that shines.
I want to have a clear mind again,
as a baby who stares at the light
wisping through the window and thinks,
That's mine.

Advice

My friend, dying, said do the hard thing first.
Always do the hard thing and you will have a better day.
The second thing will seem less hard.

She didn't tell me what to do when everything seems hard.

America Gives Israel Ten Million Dollars a Day

In jail:
Lama Khater has a two-year-old. She is not allowed to
write about politics and has been detained
7 times. The Israeli jail won't let her sleep.

Salah Hamouri is French/Palestinian, a lawyer,
detained without charges or trial for more than a year.
His house was invaded three days after he passed the bar.
Party for justice!

Mustapha Awad, Belgian artist and dancer, was crossing
the border from Jordan to visit his family's properties
when he was seized. Travel at your leisure! He does not
have a Palestinian ID.

We should all be concerned about Mohammed Zayed,
returned to prison after already serving a 19-year sentence.
No details on his new arrest, but said to be unrelated
to his first jailing. Wearing a black and white striped
French-style T-shirt in his photo, he is a Palestinian citizen
of Israel since 1948. He must be exhausted.

Who you are, exactly, or what you have been doing
all these years appears to be of little interest to Israeli
authorities when they jail you. It could be nothing.
It could be a word in a poem. Or the hand of a girl
slapping a soldier who just shot her cousin.
Wouldn't you slap him too?
Israel receives 38 billion dollars from the United
States to comfort them. Why would they care who you are?
People are jailed for pitching a stone.

Malak Mattar, a young painter of extraordinary promise,
cannot travel to France or the UK to see her exhibited work.

She knows people in those places would have welcomed her.
But some people do not want Palestinians
to "lead normal lives."
What do people in power really think about young artists?
Do they know they exist? Are artists ever normal?

And Yousef, how dare you wish to go to school?
Why should you involve yourself with student activities?
How dare you major in Electrical Engineering?
Yousef is now banned from entering
his campus. His family is "tense and frustrated."
They had already paid his fees.

I asked a rabbi demonstrating against us
if his people could imagine our sorrows.
Could they just hold their own thoughts for a moment
and imagine what we feel like?
He was quiet, staring at me.
I made a rabbi quiet.
Could he imagine the pain of the boy Ahmad Dawabsha,
only survivor of his family terribly burned
when the settlers threw a Molotov cocktail into
his house? No more mother, father, baby brother,

Ahmad, once the most beautiful little boy you can imagine,
Ahmad, now alone with sorrow and scars and pain,
wrapping his wounds. And this is what
the rabbi said: I don't know. I don't know
if we can imagine it.

And that is the problem.

Gratitude List

Thank you for insulting me.
You helped me see how much I was worth.
Thank you for overlooking my humanity.
In that moment I gained power.
To be forgotten by the wider world
and the righteous religious
and the weaponized soldiers
is not the worst thing.
It gives you time to discover yourself.

*

Lemons.
Mint.
Almonds roasted and salted.
Almonds raw.
Pistachios roasted and salted.
Cheese.

It Was or It Wasn't

Arabic fairy tales begin this way,
so do Arabic days.
A pantry is empty
but Mama still produces a tray of tea and cookies
for the guest.
West is still the way we stare—
knowing there's blue space and free water
over there. There's a Palestinian and a Jew
building a synagogue together in Arkansas.
They're friends, with respect.
Actually our water
isn't free either
nor are the fish my friends in Gaza
aren't allowed to catch.
It was or it wasn't a democracy,
a haven
for human beings,
but only some of them.
You can't do that with people,
pretend they aren't there.
It was or it wasn't a crowd.
Diploma, marriage, legacy,
babies being born,
children being killed,
it was or it wasn't going to work out.

Gaza Is Not Far Away

(Dr. Luke Peterson)

1.

It's in your cuffs.
The cup you just drank from.
Empty bucket outside back door with an inch of rain in it.
Sack of mulch to scatter on your winter beds.
Do you see these things as luxury?
It's the crosswalk kids march in.
Mama with her yellow belt
waving them through. It's rules.
It's everything you keep a long time
in your refrigerator—pickles, tonic, apple butter.
Butter. The fact you have a refrigerator
and power to run it all day long.
Gaza might like that.

2.

The world's largest open-air prison keeps ticking day to day—
alarm clocks, kindergartens, spinach mixed into eggs,
little blue backpacks for kids,
a few filtered-water fountains, plastic bottles carried home,
and no, they can't go swimming, can't fish in their own sea,
can't fly from their airport, can't visit the so-called Holy City,
can't do anything, basically, except be human, be humane.
They can go to the Book Club and read books.
And people far away won't turn their heads to see
what Gaza is doing or how well they are doing it.
Or how hard it is.
Even when 500 people die from bombs they supplied.

They won't cry because the dead ones weren't someone they knew and loved. Like the person sitting next to them on the couch.

My Wisdom

When people have a lot
they want more

When people have nothing
they will happily share it

*

Some people say
never getting your way
builds character
By now our character must be
deep and wide as a continent
Africa, Australia
giant cascade of stars
spilling over our huge night

*

Where did the power go?
Did it enjoy its break?
Is power exhausted?
What is real power?
Who really has power?
Did the generator break?
Do we imagine silence
more powerful because
it might contain everything?
Quiet always lives
inside noise.
But does it get much done?

*

Silence waits
for truth to break it

*

Calendars can weep too
They want us to have better days

*

Welcome to every minute
Feel lucky you're still in it

*

No bird builds a wall

*

Sky purse
   jingling
       change

*

Won't give up
our hopes
       for anything!

*

Not your fault
You didn't make the world

*

How dare this go on and on?
cried the person who believed in praying
God willing   God willing   God willing
There were others who prayed
     to ruins & stumps

*

Open palms
    hold more

*

Refuse to give
   mistakes
      too much power

*

Annoying person?
Person who told me to stay home
and do what other girls do?
If you disappeared
I still might miss you

*

Babies want to help us
They laugh
for no reason

*

Pay close attention to
a drop of water
on the kitchen table

*

You cannot say one word about religion
and exclude Ahmad

Each Day We Are Given So Many Gifts

I did it
I made friends with a fly

Yawn a little pause
relighting breath

Blink a break
from sun's sharp gaze

Yesterday evening after rain
the world tiled rosy

such a brief slip of minutes
as if someone got her wish

we could live in pink   hold a shining note
release   someone else's anger

Jerusalem

Not your city—
everyone's city.
Not my city—
everyone's city.

City of time—
holding time.
Deeper than time.
Time's true city.

Missing It

Our cousin Sami said at night when he can't sleep
he thinks about everything he missed that day.
Which way didn't he turn his head?
Whose face didn't he notice?
He gets the answer to the problem he missed
on the test. He finally remembers where they buried
the one cat who sat in anyone's lap.

A Person in Northern Ireland

Sends me a message with a quote
from Rainer Maria Rilke, a German poet:

"And now let us believe
in a long year that is given to us, new, untouched, full of
    things that have never been."

That's sort of what I'm afraid of.

38 Billion

It's hard to grasp very big numbers and distant concepts.
Like imagining what all our thoughts might have been
if we lived 300 years ago. Would they be centered
on a goat or six rocks piled together
or would they be wide as they are now?
In those long-ago days,
would people be meaner to one another
or nicer? I have no idea. But sometimes I wonder what
38 billion dollars could buy, instead of weapons aimed
against us and this is what comes to mind:
Eggs.   Pencils.   Undershirts of very soft cotton.
Ribbons.   Radios.   Shining flashlights.
Handmade clay plates.   Chocolates.   Really soft pillows.
Baskets.   Bracelets.   Running shoes.

Better Vision

In Ramallah, optical stores polish their glittering windows
and wait patiently, stocking shiny displays,
curatives for nearsighted, farsighted, astigmatism,
too much sun. My mother's eye swells from allergy.
Mabrook! to ourselves in the round mirrors
when suddenly the world looks sharper.
Or *Tikkun Olam*, as our Hebrew-speaking
brothers and sisters might say, repair for the world,
see close, see far, see how similar we are,
or could be, if the hatchets weren't hanging over
half our heads. Tarifi Optical, "rest your eyes from the rays,"
we'd rather rest our eyes from people who can't see us.
I'll take wide angle please, give me the whole horizon,
citizens of magnificent olive tones, curly-headed, braided,
kaftans, grandma gowns, exercise shirts, cotton dresses,
people holding hands like a children's book,
standing on the globe,
round as a floating pupil.
Tarifi Optical invites us to "swap inelegant squinting"—
I love their words, maybe I could be an optician,
focused on better sight for all, and work at the Ottica shop,
"premier inspiration destination"
for top brands of eyeglasses in the West Bank,
did you know we have such things?
People think of us differently.
We may be in prison, but we still love beauty.
We may be oppressed, but we are smart.
We may think we don't need glasses, but the big E
for equality has been lying on its back
for a long time now
kicking its legs in the air like an animal
that needs help to get up.

The Space We're In

echoes deeply
Time doesn't just crumple
the minute you turn the calendar page
I'm not sure about a country being great
I don't know what that means
It sounds like bragging or more weapons
I want a country to be nice to all people
Make them feel better
than people feel by themselves
Compassionate and gentle
I want people to
move more slowly
pay better attention
share what they have

In the old Palestinian tradition
everyone was invited in
Sit down, coffee or tea?
Mint in your tea?
Dates?
even if you didn't know the visitor

America being mean to Palestine
is nothing new
reminds me of
the dark side of junior high school
those who think you can have
only one best friend
usually end up
lonely

No Explosions

To enjoy
fireworks
you would have
to have lived
a different kind
of life

II.

EVERYTHING CHANGES

San Francisco Zen Center

Facebook Notes

Many say to Janna, Take care of yourself.
We are praying for you. Janna, you are so brave.
You run outside, our spirits go with you.

Others say you are too young to do this on your own.
Pushed forward as mouthpiece. You have charisma
so people use you as spokesperson. What's wrong

with that? A senator from Planet Young? I'll take
anyone but what we've got. Our letters to editors
trickled out for decades. What good did they do?

You are the witness, on-the-scene, microphone in
hand. You stand on the road to everywhere,
asking, *What is this? What next?*

We carry you with us wherever we go,
folded document of hope, unfolded flag,
unburdened alphabet, asking why.

Mediterranean Blue

If you are the child of a refugee, you do not
sleep easily when they are crossing the sea
on small rafts and you know they can't swim.
My father couldn't swim either. He swam through
sorrow, though, and made it to the other side
on a ship, pitching his old clothes overboard
at landing, then tried to be happy, make a new life.
But something inside him was always paddling home,
clinging to anything that floated—a story, a food, or face.
They are the bravest people on earth right now,
don't dare look down on them. Each mind a universe
swirling as many details as yours, as much love
for a humble place. Now the shirt is torn,
the sea too wide for comfort, and nowhere
to receive a letter for a very long time.

And if we can reach out a hand, we better.

To Netanyahu

My Palestinian father named his donkey after you.
Yahu—everyone thought it was for the Internet,
but he knew. Now I think he insulted the donkey.

The donkey was friends with a horse, in a field.
They didn't have much, but they shared it.
Pink flowers in spring—neither of them
tried to rule the field.

Your army just bombed a U.N. center for refugees.
Gaza, imprisoned in poverty for decades—
take that! More blood for supper.

Years since my father died,
his donkey still stands quietly
gazing from enormous eyes,
hanging his humble head.

Pharmacy

It stuns me to see the oldest man in the world buying shaving cream. He is also buying shampoo and boxed cookies, square sand tarts, a sack of chocolate peppermints. The amount of hope contained in these purchases, considering his bowed posture, his pale suit, majestic movements, his cane with a plastic coin purse attached near the handle, cannot be weighed. I think of the ten-year-old journalist photographing a demonstration of her people at home, shouting out bravely to the soldiers that threaten them, *We just want to be left alone on our land. What is wrong with being on our land?* And consider the terrain of this ancient man's own American life. Who walked it with him, who held his hand? Today he is by himself. He will step out the automatic sliding doors of the pharmacy with great effort, hauling his plastic sack of purchases, and step carefully into his car at the special marked parking place, and drive away, ever so slowly. I don't know what the little girl will do.

My Father, on Dialysis

wrote a book about Palestine called
Does the Land Remember Me?

He wrote it in longhand on scraps of paper
as his blood filtered through the big machine

He was not afraid to watch it
circulate

Nurses and aides asked him
What are you doing?

He said, planting a garden
of almonds and figs

Dipping sprigs of mint into
glasses of steaming tea

Breathing the damp stones
of my old city

Pressing my mind into the soul
of an olive tree

Blood on All Your Shirts

Even your skinny ribbed undershirt
your favorite blue guayabera
A long life of travel ends in seepage
Holes in the skin
Difficult comebacks
The graft and the duct and the valve
Flirting with nurses a hopeful distraction
Maybe they'd prick you more kindly
If you listened to their marital woes
Telling how deft and lovely they were
How ruddy their cheeks
angelic their smiles

My Immigrant Dad, On Voting

As a journalist I copied down what candidates said
But I didn't believe them
No hardly ever
If you paid attention
the people who got elected
always seemed to be crooks
after the election
Elections made me think though
At least we had them
At least people pretended
Once my friend ran for mayor and I felt excited
I know
I should have been more enthusiastic
Jimmy Carter was the only one I trusted
He saw us as human beings
He wasn't afraid to say Apartheid which of course
it was and always has been
He got in trouble for being honest
I wrote him a letter
Said he was the best president I ever had

You Are Your Own State Department

Each day I miss Japanese precision. Trying to arrange things
   the way they would. I miss the call to prayer
at Sharjah, the large collective pause. Or
the shy strawberry vendor with rickety wooden cart,
single small lightbulb pointed at a mound of berries.
   In one of China's great cities, before dawn.

   Forever I miss my Arab father's way with mint leaves
      floating in a cup of sugared tea—his delicate hands
arranging rinsed figs on a plate. What have we here?
   said the wolf in the children's story
stumbling upon people doing kind, small things.
   Is this small monster one of us?

When your country does not feel cozy, what do you do?
   Teresa walks more now, to feel closer to her
ground. If destination within two miles, she must
   hike or take the bus. Carries apples,
      extra bottles of chilled water to give away.
Kim makes one positive move a day for someone else.
I'm reading letters the ancestors wrote after arriving
   in the land of freedom, words in perfect English script . . .
describing gifts they gave one another for Christmas.
   Even the listing seems oddly civilized,
these 1906 Germans . . . *hand-stitched embroideries for dresser*
tops. Bow ties. Slippers, parlor croquet, gold ring, "pretty
   inkwell."

How they comforted themselves! A giant roast
   made them feel more at home.
      Posthumous medals of honor for
   coming, continuing—could we do that?
And where would we go?
   My father's hope for Palestine

stitching my bones, "no one wakes up and
        dreams of fighting around the house"—

someday soon the steady eyes of children in Gaza,
    yearning for a little extra electricity
to cool their lemons and cantaloupes, will be known.
            Yes?
    We talked for two hours via Google Chat,
they did not complain once. Discussing stories,
        books, families, a character who does
                what you might do.
Meanwhile secret diplomats are what we must be,
    as a girl in Qatar once assured me,
        each day slipping its blank visa into our hands.

Elementary

At the 100-year-old National Elk Refuge
near Jackson Hole, we might ask,
How long does an elk live?
Who's an old elk here?

We'd like to spend time
with an elder elk please.
Tell us how to balance our lives
on this hard edge of human mean,
mean temperatures, what we do and don't
want to mean.

Closing the door
to the news will only make you
stupid, snapped my friend
who wanted everyone to know as much
as she did. I'm hiding in old school books
with information we never used yet.
Before I drove, before I flew,
before the principal went to jail.
Sinking my eyes into tall wooden
window sashes, dreaming of light
arriving from far reaches,
our teachers as shepherds,
school a vessel of golden hope,
you could lift your daily lesson
in front of your eyes,
stare hard and think,
this will take me
somewhere. O histories of India,
geological formations of Australia,
ancient poetries of China, Japan,
someday we will be aligned in a place
of wisdom, together.

Red deer, *wapiti*, running elk rising
above yellow meadows at sundown.
An elk bows her head. In the company
of other elk, she feels at home.
And we are lost on the horizon now,
clumsy humanity,
deeper into the next century than we
can even believe,
and they will not speak to us.

On the Old Back Canal Road
by the International Hotel, Guangzhou

Janna, you are here too
everywhere
your curious thoughts
delicately constructed
You reside in every dream
of human rights
We breathe together
eating hummus made by Palestinians
where the green water weaves
between brick channels
stacked lives
laundry strung from balconies
geraniums popping red yeses
somewhere a radio playing
a very old song
three notes up and down
speaking to one another
inside the rounded mind
observatory
new and old harmonizing here
Everywhere I go
you're like the bodyguard
our slim complaints
in such a vast world
(they thought I stole the pencil box
from my room—
I had just moved it)
but no one shouting
in front of my hotel
Begone!

Gray Road North from Shenzhen

Stretching, stretching.
Sober pavement, a fog of skyscrapers,
looming gray clouds. Not one moving human
visible outside. How loud the loneliness of workers
abandoning villages for the long shifts,
disappearing into factories,
brief breaks, stark apartments
where their second pair of gray pants waits.

Stun

Who's remembering
Yemen had the most
amazing architecture
in the world?

Yemenis remember.
No one mentions this on the news.
Bomb explodes, bus
of schoolchildren.
Their glory also
unmentioned.

*

Sometimes I just call out to Dubai.
Dubai! I say. If you can build new
buildings like that,
can't you help us?

*

We stood in the parking lot
of the hospital after Daddy died.

I couldn't remember how
to open a car door.

All I Can Do

*"We have such a beautiful country, but it's not been
utilized before for this kind of tourism . . ."*
George Rishmawi, AramcoWorld

One hand out against the earth,
one hand up against the sky.

Somehow I walk between them.
They carry messages through my body,
on a cord stretched between far places.
What could have been, what might be . . .

Some days it's all I can do
to stand still and answer you.

In Some Countries

There were people who had a hundred handbags.
People who hired maids to take care of their maids.

You could float down the Rhine and see castles.
Dogs wore coats for daily walks in Central Park.

A dog's diamond collar glistened.
We were not dreaming of these things for ourselves.

We needed basics, starting small.
Hello, you look like a human being to me.

It's hard to know what open roads mean
if you've always had them.

We can't imagine
the luxury of open roads.

Seeing His Face

For Jaffar, in Dubai

When you said, first thing picking me up
at airport—*If he wins, we would have to see his face,*
hear his voice, that would be so bad for all of us—
we could still laugh. Day before election, 2016,
—surely this could not happen.

Next day, we reeled into a bright sky,
driving to a school, pummeled by morning news—
desperately you kept flicking radio stations
Arabic, English, Farsi, saying, *I'm afraid*
it just happened. How could it happen?

Shortly after, an Australian librarian
would pass me a note, *WTF?*
Small children gathering, notebooks, pencils,
how could I speak a word, now that my own country
took such a swerve? Little girls in dark uniform sweaters,
with buttons. Smiling up. Tell us where to begin.

Wales

Once a friend drove me from England into Wales for one hour's visit and that single hour was enough to suggest, for time immemorial, there are so many ways in which America can never be first. Black and white cows, nibbling gently between layered hillsides. Shocking radiance of green under silent drifting poufs. Sheep dodging up a rise, leaping alongside lined white stones. No wires, billboards, poles, not a scrap of rubbish, not a rubbish bin. Two hikers with blue backpacks lounging in a meadow. Approaching a V in the skinny one-lane pavement, my friend asked which way I wanted to turn. How would I know? Was there a preferred way? He paused. No, it is equally perfect every direction. Sorry, America. Who could say this about you?

Peace Talks

Talk
Talk
Talk
Talk
Talk
Talk
Trouble

Talk
Talk
Talk
Talk
Talk
Talk
Nothing

Freedom of Speech
(What the head-of-school told me)

We would appreciate
if you would not

(you know
in this strange climate
taking all into account
problems we have had
misunderstandings
angry parents
insults
Facebook postings
teachers being fired
demonstrations
floods)

mention the president

Jerusalem's Smile

My father speaks from the heaven
we don't believe in
Assign nothing to Jerusalem
Who is that man pretending power
over my stones?
No one with guns will ever own me
Cobbled stones feel my smile
kingdom of heaven set into sunrise
layers of giant time
They hold so many feet
tromping daily for centuries
all those bowed heads
folded hands   secret glories
are part of me
See how the man of power
stands at a podium
imagining he can say who I am
where I belong in the constellation
of cities
Trust me
I last longer than he does
shabbiest vendor
belonging to air

On the Birthday of Dr. Martin Luther King

Instead of Donald Trump, I will think of Dr. King's dignity,
his resonant voice, conviction, inclusion.

Instead of Donald Trump, I will think of Steve Ng of New Mexico,
who brought personal handmade clay cups
from his home kitchen to a writing workshop at Ghost Ranch.

Otherwise we would have been drinking
from little disposable cups.
Steve carried in two cardboard boxes, set up a table,
arranged blue, gray, elegantly designed vessels in two rows.

Pick which one you like best.

The cups helped us feel cozier, as if Ghost Ranch
could really be our home for a week.

From Steve's writing, one line:
*If I have the time to watch the shadows along the trees move, I can say I
am satisfied.*

False Alarm Hawai'i

Heavy branches, orange tangerines. Emergency alert texted to telephones throughout islands said, *Take Cover. Missile has been launched. This is not a drill.* My husband was sitting north of Honoka'a on Hawai'i Island at a table, doing his work. No television in the house. So he waited, confused. Take cover? Dive under a chair? 40 minutes till they said, *False Alarm.* In Gaza it is rarely a false alarm. It really happens. Later it is back-page news, but the schools, clinics, art centers, people are destroyed. In Honolulu, children were escorted down manholes. Hysterical students running hard along beaten gray paths at university in Manoa. I love you, I love you! Sometimes Hawai'i misses itself, true self before strip centers and public parking. It has everything it needs, but too many people want it now. Think what could be annihilated in a few seconds and has been, before. Kids at the American School in Tokyo distribute Hiroshima T-shirts before leaving on their annual Hiroshima camping trip. Who could wear it? Who could sleep?

A Palestinian Might Say

What?
You don't feel at home in your country,
almost overnight?
All the simple things
you cared about,
maybe took for granted . . .
you feel
insulted, invisible?
Almost as if you're not there?
But you're there.
Where before you mingled freely . . .
appreciated people who weren't
just like you . . .
divisions grow stronger.
That's what "chosen" and "unchosen" will do.
(Just keep your eyes on your houses and gardens.
Keep your eyes on that tree in bloom.)
Yes, a wall. Ours came later but . . .
who talks about how sad the land looks,
marked by a massive wall?
That's not a normal shadow.
It's something else looming over your lives.

Alien Rescue

1.

For years I have loved the line: *Elimination is the secret of*
chic (Balenciaga) but in the case of one's home being washed away by
mud, or storm, or Israeli bulldozer, this might not apply.

Poet Mei-mei Berssenbrugge wrote: "He says problems in Israel can be
solved by extra-terrestrials . . ."

Land here, friends. Welcome!
The Mount of Olives could use a new chapter in its story.

2.

The thing which did not go right haunts from inside
like a splinter gained from swiping a hand
across the broken chair, in sorrow.

Chair carrying echoes.

Villages humming songs of the absent ones.

Please remember we too were rooting for things to be firm.

Why is that hard to imagine?

Anthony Bourdain made everyone come to the same table.

How loud the echo right before dawn.

3.

Her voice a library of kindness.
I hear pages rustling, hungry fingers
moving through stories. If you were very alone,
you would want this voice to find you.

The Sweeper

They say she has moved to another village
to be with her cousins. Always we heard the rhythm
of brush, brush, the predictable swish of
a broom's old hairs, the straw of continuing,
yes, yes, make it better, tired but still working,
morning and evening the sweep, the rustle,
how could it be such a soft thing helped our sanity?
Litter of leaves, branch bits gathering,
she did not say goodbye.

Arab Festival T-shirt

SEATTLE 2007. I wasn't even there,
but wear this shirt proudly all the time.
Since when Arab Tragedy only? No!
Forgetting spread tables, smoky eggplant,
tiny spinach pies, punctuating pomegranate seeds,
neat almond in the center
of each rectangle of *harissa*,
since when we put down embroideries, joy,
birth certificates of stitching and knotting,
naming of constellations,
discovery of equations,
dancing with the handkerchief, oud and drum,
we will teach our children, guard our skeins
of blue and red thread,
refusing to forget laughter even if the world forgets
we ever have it
and this T-shirt with bright turquoise
and orange lettering on brave black says so.

One Small Sack in Syria

The vendor filled it fuller than it needed to be.
He wanted to make his shoppers happy.
He shook the roasted pistachios
redolent with charcoal and fire
into all corners of the brown paper bag
and smiled, folding the edge.
He said, Very good nuts.
Long road to Aleppo.
He said, Say hello to Aleppo.

Positivism

My friend in Gaza writes to me:
Gaza Strip is really so wonderful . . . regardless of the siege . . . the sea port,
the green fields, peaceful roads decorated with many red, pink, white and
orange flowering trees, decent people, elegant restaurants and hotels with
fascinating views . . . We wish . . . the crossing borders are always open
where we can travel freely and friends can come to visit us freely as well . . .

Fresh as a new notebook—that's how anyone wanted to live.

Hopeful as a pencil sharpened,
clear as one beam of light landing on the table's far side.

The children dove into a story and flew far away.

Even those who had never been to an airport
or seen a plane land at close range.

This was our superpower, retaining imagination
in worst days. They smiled shyly.

They expressed no blame.

Regret

To forgive ourselves for what we didn't do
Replay a scene over and over in mind
Change it   change
Apologizing to our own story   handful of soil
I could have planted something better here

To walk without remembering another walk
To wash off the hope of a darkened day
Make a new one

This is normal here, the fathers say
bombs exploding
tourists stepping carefully over grenades
Excuse us   this is not the life
we would have made or the way
we would have welcomed you
tear gas billowing over our streets
Regular
Usual
SOS
We are so tired

Salvation

Sitti's hands fingering red and purple velvets,
soothed by nap, by softness, pulling yellow and orange floss
snugly through, till a calm bird rises from the stitches,
with a neat knotted eye
in such hard days.

The Old Journalist Talks to Janna

From beyond the trees
I appreciate your efforts.
I see you stand, hands up, saying
Move back! to the ones with guns.
This was never easy for me to do.
After seeing them kill my friend,
I feared them. I loved my life,
did not want my mother to grieve.
You are braver than I was.
His blood spilled over the bench
where we had been sitting.

It's hard to describe how dust settles
but we all know it does.
How the bird returns to the nest
with no apology, the brother disappears
for decades, then says, *I was never mad
at anyone, I was just hurt.*
Words circulate like breezes in the evening
after a long hot day. I want to say,
Take care of yourself. We need you.
It is possible we have to be losers, dear Janna.
In the big picture who cares who won or lost?
I always thought about dignity, grace, truth.

I thought about enduring. Maybe losers
get to be taken care of!
The truth is we were so wronged and so forgotten
we had to become heroes to survive at all.
You speak the bell ringing, the wake up call,
and I am sending you the last scraps of energy
I had in my pockets when I died.

Grandfathers Say

Grandfathers say the garden is deep,
old roots twisted beyond our worry
or reach. Maybe our grief began there,
in the long history of human suffering,
where rain goes when it soaks out of sight.
Savory smoke from ancient fires
still lingers. At night you can smell it
in the stones of the walls.
When you awaken, voices
from inside your pillow
still holding you close.

The Old Journalist Writes . . .

From a notebook of Aziz Shihab

I heard my mother die.

After days of utter silence, she opened her dry toothless mouth and said,

"Aziz, let me kiss your hand. Take me on the road. Be with me on the road."

"What road?"

"It's a narrow road. The lights are strong. Green doves are flying overhead."

She said people were waiting for her on both sides of the road.

"Who are they?"

Her sister Masooda, her son, her sister Nafa, her daughter Naomi.

"But they are dead," I said.

"No, here they are," she said. "They are smiling."

She opened her eyes wider.
"Do you see them?" I asked.

"I don't see you, but I see them." She shrieked, "Stop staring at me!"

"But I'm not staring at you," I said.

"Not you. That man is staring at me, making fun of me. Go away, don't stare at me," she said again.

"Who is he?"

"A very tall man. He's pestering the little girl."

"What girl?"

"I don't know. But she is right here, sleeping next to me."

Long silence.

"Aziz, my son," she suddenly said. "Look at the grapevines.
They are loaded with sweet grapes."

"Where?"

"Right here," she said and smiled, looking up at the ceiling. "Right here."

"Hanging from the ceiling?"

"Yes."

"Hey, Masada!" she shouted. "Stay with me!"

"Were you friends with Masada before she died?"

"She didn't die. Here she is. Say hello to your Aunt Masada."

Two women came to the door of her room to visit her.
I invited them in, but she said, "No, I don't want them! They
are not from my world."

Silence. Long silence. I apologized to the women, escorted them out.

Then she fell asleep, mumbling to the little girl she said was beside her.
When she awakened she whispered, "Aziz, where are you?"

I told her I was next to her. I gently rubbed her forehead. She fell asleep again.

In less than five minutes, she awakened. "Take me home, I beg you, take me home!"

I told her she was home.

"Not this home! The one outside the gates. Right over the little shop."

I said I didn't know what she was talking about.

"Why not, son? What's wrong with you? My home outside the gate. I beg you take me home."

I told her she was a little confused.

"Oh no, I never was confused. You are. Take me home."

"Where are you now?"

"Out in the fields on the ground."

"How do you want me to take you home?"

"I'm in the water tank. I am sitting in it. Just push it."

"Does it have wheels?"

"Yes, and it is empty. Except for me."

*

She lived one more year after this.

Friend

We walked through weeds.
Two bottles pitched outside his house, boarded,
UNSAFE notice tacked to the door.

He tied an engine to a trashcan, told me to drive it.
    I did not.
You made us act in all your plays.
    I did? Who wrote the plays?
You did.
Faded curtain costumes, clink of nickels in a hat.

We're the old gang, we said to people staring.
This was our 'hood.
      You're old all right, and it ain't no more!
        Did you plant these huge leafdroppin' trees?
We curse you!
Good job, I said to my invisible
tree-planting grandpa, walking away.

Castles, fortresses, cabins.
We took note of broken twigs.
We dreamed a bear, ancient animal
come to befriend. We never fought,
could not imagine wars.
No one ever built anything lasting in the woods
so the ditch remembered us best.

Happy Birthday

Older than old people now.
Older than the auntie in the bank,
I just come in here so someone
will say Good Morning to me. Older than
the shiny-headed Englishman
at the end of the table describing his journeys
so long ago, seriously he seems like Grandpa
and you are older than he.
Paint-peeling flowerpot tipping in the grass,
faded sign for EATS, birdseed store,
they have seeds for birds you never heard of
and will scoop it into brown paper sacks to weigh
on an old-fashioned scale. Older than the scale?
Down the street everything is changing.
Abandoned factories turning to lofts.
Junior's Bar to a dental clinic.
No one cares for your opinion,
you are a rusted spike in a railroad track,
bundle of rotting leaves under the climbing rose.
Turn them under, over, be brave enough
to disappear as you promised you would
when you were young and clumsy
and strong as a roof.

Stay Afloat

What scraps we cling to these days—
giant slim stalk springing from the aloe pot,
upside-down pale orange bells
lasting for months.
Gift from the underworld.

Or Fareed Zakaria
resembling my father when I was young.
Gazing into the screen, please tell me
what is going on. Who are these strange people
we live among?

There are no olive trees or mint leaves
in their forest,
only looming bank vaults with locked drawers.
How much do they need?

Someone else will launch a bomb.
Children wake up smiling, to see their mothers killed.
How do they survive?
When I see the politicians' faces
gazing stupidly with thin smiles
as if posing
for a shaving cream ad,
I lose my mind.

Find a child to be your leader now.
Follow him through rooms, notice
his delicate moves, delight in syllables, repeat.
Announcing the swish of every passing bus.
Bow down to his love.
Babies say, *Mine, mine*, but babies are kind.

The men on the screen, jaws tight,
can't remember a single right thing to do.

To Sam Maloof's Armchair

Sam, what if we could sit in your chair an entire day,
feel its gleaming grace pervade our skin and thoughts,
would we be changed? Your walnut found a sheen
deeper than memories of women and men. You used
hand tools, liked "clean flow." When you dove
wholeheartedly into the slowness of labor's long elegance,
perfection grew. But you called yourself a "woodworker"
because it was an "honest word." The boy Sam spoke
Spanish and Arabic before English, lived among
California fruit trees, knew eight brothers and sisters.
People say you had elegant script, were always generous,
would describe to anyone how you did what you did.
A craftsman of "soul," shaping low-slung arms a sitter
might fling legs over, still feeling comfortable, calm.
Even your hinges were wood. No dazzle, no frills,
you kept shaping tables, shelves, this honorable chair
we could vote for repeatedly, timeless presence dissolving
gloom. We close our eyes, try to live in your room.

Unforgettable

In the water is a poem
unwritten by grass.
No. In the land is a poem
unwritten by water.
Everything unwritten.
Not on your forehead,
not on the sky.
The fathers sailed away
planning to return.
Not easily will they forget
a place that let us all
sorrow this much.

Rumor Mill

I heard that far away in other countries,
Finland and China, ancient Palestinian men and women
fall asleep with their hands on their hearts and by now
their hearts are shaped just like old Palestine,
not the new cut-into-bits pockmarked map of places
we are allowed to live, but the whole stitchery of towns
with melodious names, Arimathea, Bethabara,
Cana, Tiberias, Nazareth, Beersheba, Magdala,
and when these people dream, their rooms fill
with the flute music our great grandfathers loved,
the *ney*, that you used to hear around fires
at dusk, rising notes in thin curls of smoke.
Goat cheeses leavened and clarified,
small white mountains on an old black tarp.
No one had to do anything right then
but be quiet, and listen. When they awaken,
after dreaming like that, it is easier for them
to go on living.

Patience Conversations

Why don't they write about us more?

Our beauty overwhelms them.

Why can't they hear our worlds echoing back and forth?

Song with doubled harmony. Ears closed.

Who wanted what?

We all love falafel.

Calling us anti-Semitic

when we are Semites too,

no joke, no one is laughing.

Why don't they ask the right questions?

What's hard for you? That's hard for me too.

Why do they stare at us as if they never saw kids before?

Where are their memories?

Have they placed their memories in iron lock boxes
buried in the cement of the drainage ditch?

Do they see the kids who have to walk to school
through the drainage ditch?

Because they won't let them cross the road?

Tell my story, tell my story.

Memory was always staring hard at itself
inside my head.

Does the wide world know there are two roads,
one for them and one for us? And ours isn't good?

The wide world! Singing of the stable and the cows.
Donkey and kings. Wise men.
We would be so happy to meet.

Pothole, crack. Pothole, crack.

Where were the wise women?
Children circling, chanting in the shadow of the wall.
Small boy carrying broken candle
he found on the ground. Not even a wick left.
Doing the dust dance.
Kicking the foot.
We were waiting.

Living

On the last day of the world
I would want to plant a tree
　　　　　—W. S. Merwin

Never wanted to think about
the last day of the world

Do these palms think about it?
That sea? Wedge of blue under blue?

You can't be sure of anything now
Sound waves rolling

Finally understanding a phrase
Sitting on hillside in garden

You don't have to say anything
for conversation to exist

Tiny Journalist Blues

Nothing to give you
that you would want.

Nothing big enough
but freedom.

Acknowledgments

Grateful acknowledgment is made to the editors of the following publications in which these poems first appeared, some in different versions:

ARC (Canada): "Jerusalem's Smile";
The Horn Book Magazine: "Exotic Animals, Book for Children";
Manoa: "On the Old Back Canal Road by the International Hotel,
     Guangzhou," "Gray Road North from Shenzhen";
Massachusetts Review: "To Netanyahu";
Plough: "Gaza Is Not Far Away";
Poetrybay: "'ISRAEL LETS BULLDOZERS GRIND TO HALT.'"

"Mediterranean Blue" was originally published in *Traveling the Blue Road: Poems of the Sea* (Seagrass Press, 2017), edited by Lee Bennett Hopkins, and *Making Mirrors: Righting/Writing by Refugees* (Olive Branch Press, 2018), edited by Jehan Bseiso and Becky Thompson.

"You Are Your Own State Department" was originally published in *Healing the Divide: Poems of Kindness and Connection* (Green Writers Press, 2019), edited by James Crews.

"Freedom of Speech" and "Wales" were originally published in *Drunk in a Midnight Choir* (CreateSpace, 2015), edited by Todd Gleason.

"To Sam Maloof's Armchair" appeared in the Dallas Museum of Art newsletter.

"Jerusalem" was partial text for *Al-Quds: Jerusalem*, an oratorio composed by Mohammed Fairouz and performed at the Metropolitan Museum of Art, New York City, 2016.

With gratitude to Peter Conners, Michael Nye, Miriam Shihab, Ryushin Paul Haller and Tassajara, Eliza Fischer, Steven Barclay, Virginia Duncan, Patrick Lannan and the Lannan Foundation, Carol

Kwehock, Marjorie Ransom, Deborah Pope, Konrad Ng, Shangri La and the Doris Duke Foundation for Islamic Arts, Seeds of Peace, for continuing to believe, Debra Sugerman, for her unforgettable films "Dear Mr. President" and "Broken," and Creativity for Peace camp, Dr. Mazin Qumsiyeh of Bethlehem and cyberspace, Sani Meo, Ibtisam Barakat, The NSK Neustadt Prize for Children's Literature, all my sister and brother Arab American writers, our Jewish sisters and brothers who work toward equality and justice, Libby and Len Traubman, my late father Aziz Shihab, author of *Does the Land Remember Me? A Memoir of Palestine*, (Syracuse University Press), my grandmother Sitti Khadra Shihab Idais Al-Zer, who lived steadily under West Bank occupation, near Janna's village, until age 106, The Arab American National Museum in Dearborn, Michigan, and our beloved friend Kathleen Sommers of San Antonio, for longtime support and encouragement.

Anthony Bourdain, we wish you had lived forever.

Peace, peace, said all three religions.
They said that. Then?
Our footsteps echoed in the ancient streets.

"It is a shameful moment for US media when it insists on being subservient to the grotesque propaganda agencies of a violent, aggressive state."
—Noam Chomsky

Tell our story, tell our story.

About the Author

Naomi Shihab Nye joined Facebook to follow Janna. She wishes American politicians would "follow" Janna so they might be better aware of how their money is spent. Janna's calm and curiosity remind Nye of her father Aziz Shihab, born in Jerusalem in 1927, employed by the BBC while yet a teen—always a believer in getting facts and truth "out there." Aziz would become a lifelong journalist as Naomi became a lifelong creative writer, publishing her first poems at age seven, the same age when Janna started posting videos. Currently on faculty at Texas State University, Naomi is recipient of the Lon Tinkle Award for Lifetime Achievement from the Texas Institute of Letters.

BOA Editions, Ltd., American Poets Continuum Series

Colophon

BOA Editions, Ltd., a not-for-profit publisher of poetry and other literary works, fosters readership and appreciation of contemporary literature. By identifying, cultivating, and publishing both new and established poets and selecting authors of unique literary talent, BOA brings high-quality literature to the public. Support for this effort comes from the sale of its publications, grant funding, and private donations.

The publication of this book is made possible, in part, by the support of the following individuals:

Anonymous
Anonymous, *in memory of Aziz Shihab*
Angela Bonazinga & Catherine Lewis
Susan Burke & Bill Leonardi, *in honor of Boo Poulin*
Rome Celli
Peter & Aimee Conners
Suressa & Richard Forbes
Robert L. Giron
James Long Hale
Jack & Gail Langerak
Melanie & Ron Martin-Dent
Joe McElveney
Boo Poulin
Deborah Ronnen
Steven O. Russell & Phyllis Rifkin-Russell
Robert Thomas
William Waddell & Linda Rubel
Michael Waters & Mihaela Moscaliuc